DISCOVER!

PEOPLE of the PAST

WHO WAS BENJAMIN FRANKLIN?

Robert Clore

Enslow PUBLISHING

Please visit our website, www.enslow.com. For a free color catalog of all our high-quality books, call toll free 1-800-398-2504 or fax 1-877-980-4454.

Cataloging-in-Publication Data
Names: Clore, Robert.
Title: Who was Benjamin Franklin? / Robert Clore.
Description: Buffalo, NY : Enslow Publishing, 2027. | Series: People of the past | Includes glossary.
Identifiers: ISBN 9781978550476 (pbk.) | ISBN 9781978550483 (library bound) | ISBN 9781978550490 (ebook)
Subjects: LCSH: Franklin, Benjamin, 1706-1790–Juvenile literature. | Statesmen–United States–Biography–Juvenile literature. | Scientists–United States–Biography–Juvenile literature. | Inventors–United States–Biography–Juvenile literature. | Printers–United States–Biography–Juvenile literature.
Classification: LCC E302.6.F8 C657 2027 | DDC 973.3092 B–dc23

Published in 2027 by
Enslow Publishing
2544 Clinton Street
Buffalo, NY 14224

Designer: Claire Vanden Branden
Editor: Max Pritchard

Photo Credits: Cover, p. 1 Everett Collection/Shutterstock.com; pp. 5, 9 Library of Congress; p. 7 Wikimedia Commons; p. 11 New York Public Library; p. 13 Fer Gregory/Shutterstock.com; p. 15 The White House Historical Association; p. 17 Smithsonian Institution; p. 19 Henry Hintermeister/Library of Congress; p. 21 Elena Belgo/ Shutterstock.com.

Printed in China

CPSIA compliance information: Batch #QS27ENS: For further information contact Enslow Publishing, at 1-800-398-2504.

CONTENTS

FOUNDING FATHER....................4
EARLY LIFE 6
BUSINESSMAN 10
ELECTRIC EXPERIMENT.........12
GOVERNMENT WORK...............14
A NEW NATION........................18
A LASTING LEGACY 20
GLOSSARY...............................22
FOR MORE INFORMATION 23
INDEX......................................24

BOLDFACE WORDS APPEAR IN THE GLOSSARY.

FOUNDING FATHER

Benjamin Franklin was one of the Founding Fathers of the United States. Benjamin is sometimes called Ben for short. He helped 13 British colonies become the United States. Ben was a writer, a **diplomat**, and an inventor.

EARLY LIFE

Ben was born January 17, 1706. He was one of 17 children! The family lived in Boston, Massachusetts. Ben didn't go to school for very long. He read a lot and taught himself to write well. By age 12, he was working for his brother's newspaper.

[N° 1]

THE New-England Courant.

MONDAY August 7. 1721.

Homo non unius Negotii: Or, *Jack of all Trades.*

Mr John Checkley

IT'S an hard Case, that a Man can't appear in Print now a Days, unless he'll undergo the Mortification of Answering to ten thousand senseless and Impertinent Questions like these, Pray Sir, from whence came you? And what Age may you be of, may I be so bold? Was you bred at Colledge Sir? And can you (like some of them) square the Circle, and cypher as far as the Black Art? &c. *Now, tho' I must confess it's something irksome to a Man in hast, thus to be stop'd at his first setting-out, yet in Compliance to the Custom of the Country where I now set up for an Author, I'll immediately stop short, and give my gentle Reader some Account of my Person and my rare Endowments.*

As for my Age, I'm some odd Years and a few Days under twice twenty and three, *therefore I hope no One will hereafter object against my soaring now and then with the* grave Wits *of the Age, since I have dropt my callow Feathers, and am pretty well fledg'd: but if they should tell me that I am not yet fit nor worthy to keep Company with such* Illustrious Sages, *for my Beard do's n't yet reach down to my Girdle, I shall make them no other Answer than this,* Barba non facit Philosophum.

I make no Question my gentle Readers, but that you're

Dr Douglass

abnormis sapiens.—— Hor.

At the Request of several Gentlemen in Town:
A Continuation of the History of Inoculation in *Boston*,
by a Society of the Practitioners in Physick.

THe bold undertaker of the Practice of the Greek old Women, notwithstanding the Terror and Confusion from his Son's Inoculation-Fever, proceeds to inoculate Persons from Seventy Years of Age and downwards.

The Select Men (or Managers of the Town Affairs) in duty bound to take Cognizance of the Matter, desire a Meeting of all the Practitioners in Town, to have their Opinion whether the Practice ought to be allowed or not; *they unanimously agreed that is was rash and dubious*, being entirely new, not in the least vouched or recommended (being meerly published, in the Philosophick Transactions by way of Amusement) from Britain, tho' it came to us *via* London from the Turks, and by a strong *viva voce* Evidence, *was proved to be of fatal & dangerous Consequence. B——n* is desired by the Select Men to desist.

Notwithstanding the general Aversion of the Town, *in Contradiction* to the declared Opinion of the Practitioners, *in Opposition* to the Selectmen, and *in Spite* of the discouraging Evidences relating to this Practice, *Six Gentlemen of Piety and Learning, profoundly igno-*

Ben moved to Philadelphia, Pennsylvania, when he was 17. He worked as a printer. Then, Ben went to London, England. He returned to Philadelphia in 1726. He married Deborah Read Rogers in 1730. The couple had two children. Their son, Franky, passed away at the age of four. Their daughter, Sarah, became a leading **patriot** in the American Revolution.

SOUTH MARKET
Wm BRADFORD
PRINTING OFFICE
LONDON COFFEE HOUSE

BUSINESSMAN

By the age of 42, Ben had become rich enough to retire from work. He had been the official printer of Philadelphia's paper money. He published *Poor Richard's Almanack*. This yearly book had a calendar and weather predictions. After retiring, Ben purchased enslaved people. He later spoke out against slavery.

Poor Richard, 1733.

AN

Almanack

For the Year of Chriſt

1733,

Being the Firſt after LEAP YEAR.

And makes ſince the Creation	Years
By the Account of the Eaſtern *Greeks*	7241
By the Latin Church, when ☉ ent. ♈	6932
By the Computation of *W.W.*	5742
By the *Roman* Chronology	5682
By the *Jewiſh* Rabbies.	5494

ELECTRIC EXPERIMENT

Ben now had time to pursue his many interests. He helped establish a public library and firefighting company in Philadelphia. Ben also studied electricity. He learned many new things about it. He used a kite and a key to prove that lightning is made of electricity. The **experiment** was very dangerous.

GOVERNMENT WORK

Ben served in the Philadelphia city government during the 1740s and 1750s. He hoped to rise to political power in England. However, by the 1760s, many **colonists** were angry with British laws. Ben wrote **essays** about the colonists' problems.

BENJAMIN FRANKLIN, 1767

In 1776, Ben helped write the **Declaration of Independence**. He was then sent to be the US diplomat to France. Ben was very popular there. He asked the French to help the colonists fight British rule. He convinced the French to send money and military support.

A NEW NATION

In 1783, the United States won its independence! Ben helped work out a peace agreement with England. Then, he helped pass the **US Constitution** in 1787.

A LASTING LEGACY

Ben died in 1790. However, his work lives on. Ben invented many things, including a special kind of glasses and a stove. He now appears on the $100 bill. Today, he is remembered for his inventions, his life story, and for helping shape the United States.

of the United States.
100
100
100
100
RESERVE SYSTEM
E2
D4
pursuing invariably the same Object

GLOSSARY

colonists: People who live in a colony, or a piece of land under the control of another country.

Declaration of Independence: The piece of writing that stated the colonies' wish to form their own government without British control.

diplomat: A person who handles talks about political issues between nations.

essays: Pieces of writing about a subject that share a writer's ideas.

experiment: A test that tries out a new idea.

patriot: A colonist who rebelled against British control during the American Revolution.

US Constitution: The piece of writing stating the rules of the United States government.

FOR MORE INFORMATION

Books

Sherman, Suzanne. *The Shocking Story of Electricity*. New York, NY: DK Publishing, 2023.

Woelfle, Gretchen. *How Benjamin Franklin Became a Revolutionary in Seven (Not-So-Easy) Steps*. New York, NY: Astra Books, 2023.

Websites

Britannica Kids: Benjamin Franklin
kids.britannica.com/kids/article/Benjamin-Franklin/353147
Learn about Ben Franklin's life and see historical images.

GPO: Benjamin Franklin
bensguide.gpo.gov/about-ben-and-gpo
Read more about Ben Franklin's inventions and how his work led to the US Government Printing Office (GPO).

Publisher's note to educators and parents: Our editors have carefully reviewed these websites to ensure that they are suitable for students. Many websites change frequently, however, and we cannot guarantee that a site's future contents will continue to meet our high standards of quality and educational value. Be advised that students should be closely supervised whenever they access the internet.

INDEX

Boston, 6
colonists, 14, 16
Declaration of
  Independence, 16
diplomats, 4, 16
electricity, 12
England, 8, 18
Founding Fathers, 4
France, 16
inventing, 4, 20
libraries, 12
London, 10
Philadelphia, 8, 10, 12, 14
printing, 8, 10
Rogers, Deborah Read,
  10
schooling, 6
United States, 4, 18, 20
US Constitution, 18
writing, 4